Chains *to* Change

Breaking Trauma and Building Healthy Relationships

J. LOVE

Chains to Change: Breaking Trauma and Building Healthy Relationships

This book is a work of nonfiction. Some names and identifying details have been changed to protect privacy.

Scripture quotations are from the Holy Bible, King James Version (KJV), unless otherwise noted.

Printed in the United States of America

ISBN: 979-8-9953272-1-9

Editing, cover design, and interior formatting by Buckingham Press

Dedication

This book is dedicated to everyone who has ever been broken, betrayed, or bruised by life—and still found the courage to keep going.

To the men and women who silently carry childhood trauma, heartbreak, and disappointment, yet continue to show up for others even when you struggle to show up for yourself—this is for you.

To my family, whose love gave me strength when I felt unworthy. And to those who doubted me, rejected me, or turned their backs on me—you, too, shaped this journey. Your absence taught me the power of presence, and your betrayal taught me the value of trust.

Most importantly, this book is dedicated to my mother, who is also my best friend and Queen. Thank you for always loving me unconditionally. You never gave up on me, and your love helped me transform my pain into peace.

Table of Contents

Foreword

There are some stories that you read—and others that you feel. *Chains to Change: Breaking Trauma and Building Healthy Relationships* is one of those rare works that does both. It grips your heart and speaks directly to the part of you that has been bruised by life but still believes in healing.

As a licensed clinical psychotherapist, and empathy and resilience expert who has spent more than two decades supporting others in facing pain, I know that healing doesn't begin in an office. It begins in honesty—the moment you stop pretending and finally say, *"I'm not fine, but I want to be."* This book captures that moment.

What makes this work powerful is not just its transparency but its transformation. J. Love does not write from the comfort of completion; he writes from the middle of becoming. That is where real healing lives—in the messy, uncertain, courageous space between who you were and who you are still trying to be. Through each chapter, he invites readers to sit in that tension and do the sacred work of turning wounds into wisdom.

I was deeply moved by the courage it takes to write openly about childhood trauma, abuse, shame, incarceration, and faith. These are not easy topics. Yet instead of sensationalizing the pain, J Love uses it as a mirror, allowing readers to see their own reflections in his story. He shows that brokenness is not the end of the road but often the doorway to breakthrough.

In a world that glorifies perfection and hides pain, *Chains to Change* is an act of rebellion and redemption. It reclaims vulnerability as strength. It reminds us that the greatest victories are often born from the most devastating losses. It teaches that we are not what happened to us—we are what we choose to do with it.

This book is more than a memoir; it is a manual for healing. Each reflection journal at the end of the chapter functions like a mirror, calling you to pause, look inward, and participate in your own recovery. It blends the rawness of real-life struggle with the principles of emotional, spiritual, and psychological growth. It is as much about restoration as it is about redemption.

Whether you are reading this as a counselor, a believer, a parent, or simply a human being navigating pain, you will find yourself somewhere in these pages. You will see that trauma does not have to be a life sentence. You will discover that forgiveness—of self and others—is the key to freedom. And you will remember that peace is not found in the absence of problems but in the presence of purpose.

I often tell my clients that healing requires three things: **empathy, resilience, and transformation**. This book embodies all three. It is empathy in print, resilience in testimony, and transformation in motion.

So, before you turn the page, I invite you to read with your heart open. Let these words challenge you, comfort you, and call you higher. Let them remind you that every scar carries a story—and every story, when healed, can set someone else free.

May this book be a mirror for reflection, a manual for growth, and a ministry of hope. And may you, like the author, find the courage to turn your own chains into change.

With empathy and resilience,
Dr. Dwayne L. Buckingham, Ph.D., LCSW-C, BCD
The E.R. Doctor™ — Empathy & Resilience Doctor

Introduction

"Healing begins where the mask ends."
— Dr. Dwayne L. Buckingham.

Affirmation:
I am ready to face my truth, not to relive my pain, but to release it.

We all carry scars. Some are visible, others are buried deep within our hearts. For years, I carried mine silently—childhood trauma, abuse, abandonment, betrayal, broken relationships, and the weight of mistakes I thought would define me forever.

Like many people, I tried to cope in unhealthy ways. I masked my pain with women, gambling, and pride. I wore toughness like armor, convincing the world I was fine, even when I was falling apart inside. I thought money, status, or sex would heal me. They didn't. They only made me emptier.

It wasn't until I hit rock bottom—sitting in prison, stripped of my freedom and everything I thought gave me value—that I realized healing had to come from within. It wasn't something I could buy, borrow, or fake. Healing had to be intentional. It had to be spiritual. It had to start with honesty.

This book is my testimony and my offering. It's written from a place of process, not perfection. I am still healing, learning, becoming. My hope is that by sharing my story—the good, the bad, and the broken—you will see pieces of your own journey and find the courage to begin or continue your healing process.

Inside these chapters, you'll find my reflections on childhood trauma, depression, brokenness, trust, sex, self-esteem, boundaries, and faith. But this isn't just about me. It's about you. As you read, I encourage you to pause often, reflect on your own experiences, and ask yourself the questions at the end of each chapter. Healing is not passive. It is active, and it requires your participation.

If you take nothing else from this book, take this: **you are not your past. You are not your pain. You are not your mistakes.** Healing is possible. Love is possible. Peace is possible.

This is the beginning of that journey. Let's walk it together.

CHAPTER 1

Childhood Trauma

"He heals the brokenhearted and binds up their wounds." — Psalm 147:3 (NIV)

Affirmation:
My past shaped me, but it does not define me.
I am rewriting my story.

Healing is not a quick fix, but a process that can take time—weeks, months, or even years—depending on your commitment. Making it a daily practice brings peace and growth. For many, our deepest wounds trace back to childhood. We may not realize our struggles as adults connect to our earliest experiences. I encourage those on this journey to seek out self-help resources like Healing the Child Within and spiritual guidance. For me, reading the Bible and reconnecting with God were essential. My favorite scripture is Revelation 13:9-10: "Whenever I am weary, lean on God because He has the answers we seek, and His strength often shows up in our weakest moments."

Growing Up in Chaos

I grew up in a neighborhood where drugs were everywhere. Crack cocaine, heroin, and pills weren't hidden—they were out in the open. Drug addicts used in front of us. Violence was part of everyday life. Shootings and robberies weren't shocking—they were normal. To us kids, being a gangster seemed cool because the people we looked up to were the same people destroying our community.

The men I admired—my uncles and older cousins—treated women as objects. They had multiple side pieces and mistresses, and I never once saw them honor faithfulness. Without realizing it, I copied what I saw. By the time I entered relationships, I was repeating their same broken patterns.

I didn't have a father in the home. My mother raised my younger sister and me until she started dating seriously when I was eight. By then, I was already influenced by the streets. My father had died, and in my mind, I had to carry his legacy. People in the neighborhood would tell me, *"You're going to be just like your pops. He ran his hood. He got money. He was a legend."*

That pressure shaped me in ways I didn't understand at the time.

Loss, Pressure, and Pain

As a child, I lost people close to me. At seven years old, my godbrother Donovan—my best friend—died. Not long after, my great-grandmother passed away. Death became a constant presence in my life. On top of that, I saw men I admired—uncles, friends, neighbors—come and go in and out of prison. Losing people to death or incarceration hardened me. I became angry with the world and, at times, even with God.

But nothing affected me more than the abuse I experienced. Between ages seven and ten, I was molested by two different women—both older family friends. They made me do things no child should ever have to endure. I kept it secret because in my neighborhood, "snitching" was forbidden. That silence shaped me. I became overly sexual at a young age, trying to mimic what had been done to me. When my mother asked where I learned it, I never told her. Shame and fear silenced me.

Armor and Anger

In the hood, showing emotions was seen as a weakness. Crying or admitting hurt made you soft. So I buried my feelings. I wore an armor of toughness to hide my pain. On the outside, I was hard. On the inside, I was broken.

I lashed out in the streets—angry, reckless, and self-destructive. Sports had once been my ticket out. I had Division 1 and 2 football scholarships lined up by ninth grade. But instead of pursuing them, I chased fast money, drugs, and the streets. That path led me in and out of juvenile centers until, eventually, I was sentenced to life without parole.

Looking back, I see how childhood trauma shaped almost every choice I made. The absence of a father, the pressure of expectations, the pain of molestation, and the constant loss of loved ones all piled up inside me. With no safe space to release it, I carried it into every relationship and decision.

Lessons for Healing

Childhood trauma can affect us for decades. It influences the way we love, trust, and parent. Many people repeat the cycles they witnessed as children because they never heal from them. Parents who were abused often become abusers. Kids who felt abandoned often grow into adults who fear rejection or sabotage relationships.

If you are a parent, be mindful of the pressure you put on your children. Words that seem small to you can leave heavy scars on them. If you are still carrying childhood pain, know that silence only deepens the wound. Healing starts with honesty—with yourself and with someone safe enough to confide in.

As Dr. Bessel van der Kolk explains in *The Body Keeps the Score*, trauma lives in the body. It doesn't just go away. It shows up in depression, addiction, anger, or broken relationships until we confront it.

Reflection for the Reader

- What unspoken pains from your childhood still affect you today?
- Were you ever pressured to "be strong" instead of expressing your emotions?

- How might your upbringing be influencing the way you treat yourself and others right now?

Closing Thought

My story is filled with loss, abuse, and mistakes, but it is also filled with lessons. If you recognize parts of yourself in my experiences, know this—you are not alone, and you are not beyond healing. Your childhood does not define your future. Healing is possible.

Childhood Trauma – Reflection Journal

1. Looking Back:

What is your earliest memory of feeling unsafe, unseen, or unloved? How did that shape your sense of trust and safety?

2. Emotional Armor:

When did you first learn that showing emotion could be dangerous or "weak"? How does that belief affect your relationships today?

3. Healing Dialogue:

Write a short letter to your younger self. What would you tell that child about safety, love, and worthiness?

4. Faith & Recovery:

How can you invite faith or spirituality into your healing process in a way that feels real, not forced?

CHAPTER 2

Being Broken

"Out of suffering have emerged the strongest souls; the most massive characters are seared with scars." — Kahlil Gibran

Affirmation:
I may be broken, but I am still breathing—and that means I am still becoming.

Depression doesn't always come from the obvious places. For me, it wasn't just about being incarcerated—it was about losing my identity when I lost my money.

I had hustled for two years, stacking more than $50,000. I was on a winning streak with FanDuel, and for the first time, I felt like freedom was within reach. That money was supposed to secure the lawyer I believed could get me home. Then, with one phone call, it was gone. The woman I trusted to hold it had spent everything. Just like that, my dreams and savings disappeared.

I can still remember the emptiness that settled over me. It wasn't just the money—it was that my entire identity had become tied to it. Without money, I felt like nothing. I chased my losses through more gambling, desperate to get it back, but all I did was dig myself deeper.

Three months later, sitting in segregation—the hole—I opened my Bible. That was the first time in years I felt even a glimmer of peace. That's also where the idea for this book was born.

Coping the Wrong Way

When broken, people cope in different ways. I chased affection, convincing myself that women could fill the emptiness inside me. I wasn't trying to be a womanizer, but my actions made me one. I entertained multiple women, lying to each of them just to feel wanted for a moment.

It wasn't love. It wasn't even a connection. It was selfishness. I was too consumed with my own pain to notice how I was hurting others. One heartbreak made me care even less. I convinced myself that all women were the same, searching for flaws that weren't there.

Eventually, I realized that I wasn't just damaging others—I was damaging myself. I was blocking blessings, ruining relationships, and becoming numb.

The Darkest Place

My depression deepened until I even considered suicide. I started to believe the judge's words—that I was a menace, that I deserved to be here forever. I thought maybe all the pain I felt was karma for the wrong I'd done.

Depression is like a storm of lies. It tells you that you're worthless, unlovable, and alone. Some days I couldn't even get out of bed. It felt like demons were playing with my thoughts.

If you've ever been there, you know it's not about weakness—it's about being overwhelmed. Even the strongest people break when the weight is too heavy.

Recognizing the Emotions of the Broken

When a man is broken, he carries a dangerous mix of emotions:

- Loneliness
- Self-pity
- Suicidal thoughts
- Desperation
- Anger and frustration
- A constant sense of failure

I lived every one of those feelings. And the more I chased temporary satisfaction—women, money, gambling—the emptier I felt. Healing only began when I looked in the mirror and admitted, "I am the problem." *My choices have led me here.*

Lessons From the Darkness

I've been incarcerated since I was 18 years old. Over the years, I've met women from every background—professionals, hustlers, dreamers, survivors. At first, I lied, cheated, and disrespected them. But eventually, I started to learn.

Life has a way of holding up a mirror. Every deceitful thing I did came back to me. Every lie I told found its way into my own life. That's the law of the universe—you reap what you sow.

The most important realization? I wasn't ready for real love because I didn't love myself. I kept settling, thinking I could mold women into what I wanted. But I am not God. I had to stop forcing relationships and start working on myself.

Reflection for the Reader

- Have you ever tied your identity to money, status, or relationships? What happened when those things failed you?
- Do you find yourself chasing temporary comfort—sex, drugs, gambling, or distractions—instead of facing your pain?
- What emotions from the list above do you recognize in yourself right now?

Closing Thought

Being broken doesn't make you less human—it makes you real. But staying broken is a choice. Healing begins when we stop running, take accountability, and let God restore what pain has destroyed.

If you are feeling suicidal or overwhelmed, please know this: you are enough. Seek help. Talk to someone you trust. And most importantly, remember—your story isn't finished yet.

Being Broken – Reflection Journal

1. Identity & Loss:

What have you tied your self-worth to—money, success, appearance, or relationships? What would it look like to find value beyond those things?

2. Facing Darkness:

When was the last time you felt hopeless or deeply depressed? How did you respond, and what helped you endure?

3. Emotional Coping:

What coping mechanisms do you use when you're hurt or disappointed? Which of them brings healing—and which brings more pain?

4. Spiritual Reframe:

If your brokenness had a message for you, what would it say?

CHAPTER 3

The Beginning of Healing

"Create in me a clean heart, O God; and renew a right spirit within me." — Psalm 51:10 (KJV)

Affirmation:
I no longer run from my pain; I sit with it until it teaches me peace.

When life breaks us, it's tempting to believe that money, status, or material things will fix the pain. But I learned the hard way—none of those things can heal you. They may distract you for a moment, but the wounds remain. Healing doesn't come from the outside. It begins within.

Facing the Root of the Hurt

The first step in healing is honesty. You have to be willing to identify the root of your pain, even if it's uncomfortable. For me, that meant admitting that my happiness was tied to other people's opinions, to money, and to arrogance.

I didn't come to that realization on my own. It took a woman who listened closely to my complaints and frustrations to reflect the truth back to me. She showed me that my foundation was built on pride and brokenness. That relationship ended painfully, but it was also the turning point. Sometimes God uses people to expose what we cannot see in ourselves.

Healing begins when we stop running, stop hiding, and start telling the truth about what is really hurting us.

Transformation and Growth

Dr. Na'im Akbar, in his book *New Visions for Black Men*, compares the transformation of a caterpillar to the transformation of human beings. A caterpillar that doesn't enter the cocoon eventually dies because it never fulfills its purpose. In the same way, if we refuse to go through our own process of healing and growth, we remain trapped in cycles of dysfunction.

Healing is our cocoon. It's where the pain we've endured transforms into wisdom and strength. But the process requires courage—it requires us to shed the armor and face what's inside.

Accountability: Who to Blame?

One of the hardest truths to accept is that many of our problems are not caused by others—they are caused by us. For years, I blamed the world, my environment, and the people who hurt me. But part of healing is taking responsibility.

That doesn't mean victims of abuse are to blame for their pain. But it does mean that we have to acknowledge where our own decisions contributed to our struggles. Denial keeps us stuck; accountability sets us free.

Healing comes when we can say, "Yes, I was wrong." *Yes, I made poor choices. But I am willing to change.*

Faith as a Foundation

Healing is not only psychological; it's spiritual. Faith carried me when nothing else could. In my weakest moments—when I doubted my worth and questioned my purpose—it was faith that reminded me I was still here for a reason.

Faith doesn't remove fear. It gives you the strength to move forward in spite of it. When you believe that God has a plan bigger than your pain, you find the courage to keep going.

Practical Steps for Healing

Here are a few steps that guided me when my own healing began:

1. **Ask hard questions.** Be honest about your upbringing, your trauma, and the habits you've carried into adulthood.
2. **Seek outside perspectives.** Let trusted friends or family tell you where you need to grow. Don't get defensive—listen.
3. **Acknowledge patterns.** Notice the cycles you repeat in relationships, choices, and emotions.

4. **Take accountability.** Stop pointing fingers at everyone else. Own your role.
5. **Trust the process.** Healing is not overnight. It is daily work.

Reflection for the Reader

- What root causes of pain have you been avoiding?
- Are there areas where you blame others, but deep down know you need to take responsibility?
- How would your life look different if you truly committed to healing?

Closing Thought

Healing is not about becoming perfect. It is about becoming whole. It requires honesty, accountability, and faith. It asks us to enter the cocoon of self-reflection and transformation, even when it feels unbearable.

The beginning of healing is simply this: the decision to stop running and to face yourself. Once you do, peace will no longer be a stranger—it will become your companion.

The Beginning of Healing – Reflection Journal

1. Radical Honesty:

What truth about yourself have you been avoiding? Why?

2. Accountability Check:

List three choices you've made that contributed to your pain—and three new choices that could move you toward healing.

3. Cocoon Moment:

Describe what your "cocoon phase" looks like right now—what are you shedding, and what are you becoming?

4. Faith Reflection:

Write a prayer, affirmation, or meditation that anchors your healing journey.

CHAPTER 4

Pieces of Armor

"We wear masks to survive, and then forget to take them off to live." — Dr. Dwayne L. Buckingham

Affirmation:

My strength is not in my armor, but in my ability to be real.

As children, we learn to protect ourselves. When something hurts us—whether it's rejection, abuse, or disappointment—we create defense mechanisms. I call these our *pieces of armor.* At first, armor feels like survival. It shields us from pain, embarrassment, or vulnerability. But as we grow older, the armor can become so heavy that we lose sight of who we truly are. Healing means learning when to put the armor down.

The Armor of Toughness

Growing up in the neighborhood I did, toughness wasn't optional—it was a requirement. To survive, I learned to hide my feelings behind a mask of aggression and fearlessness. On the outside, I looked hard. On the inside, I was hurting.

The armor protected me from being seen as weak, but it also cost me. It pushed people away. It made me numb to opportunities for love and trust. Many of us carry this same armor—presenting strength while silently bleeding.

Ego and Pride

Two of the most common pieces of armor are ego and pride. They hide our insecurities, but at a high cost.

Ego tells us we're above correction. Pride convinces us we don't need help. Together, they keep us trapped. For years, my pride ruined relationships. I pushed people away rather than admit I was wrong. I wore arrogance like a crown, but it was really just a mask for my fear of being seen as inadequate.

The truth is, ego and pride are fragile shields. When life knocks you down—and it will—they shatter, leaving you more exposed than ever.

The Armor of Emotional Numbness

Some people wear armor by becoming emotionless. After being hurt too many times, they decide, *"I won't feel anymore."*

I understand this armor. I wore it myself. I wanted people to think I didn't care about anything. That image gave me power on the streets, but it made me lonely in real life. Being emotionless may protect you temporarily, but it also keeps love, joy, and healing at a distance.

The Armor of Repressed Anger

Another dangerous form of armor is repressed anger. When we're taught not to cry or express hurt, those feelings don't disappear—they build up inside. Eventually, they explode as rage, violence, or bitterness.

As a child, I often bottled up my pain. I resented not having what other kids had, but I didn't want to hurt my mother by saying it. That repression turned into anger at the world. Many of us still carry unspoken childhood frustrations that surface in our adult relationships.

Recognizing and Releasing the Armor

The problem with armor is that the longer we wear it, the more we confuse it with our identity. We start to believe we *are* the toughness, the pride, the anger. But those are only shields—pieces of unhealed trauma.

Healing requires us to take the armor off, piece by piece. It's not easy. You may feel naked without it. But underneath, you'll rediscover who you really are.

Reflection for the Reader

- What "armor" do you wear to protect yourself—anger, pride, numbness, toughness?

- How has that armor protected you in the past? How has it harmed you in the present?
- Who in your life gets to see you without your armor?

Closing Thought

Armor can keep us safe, but it can also keep us stuck. Healing means finding the courage to lay it down, trusting that vulnerability is not weakness—it's the first step toward freedom.

Pieces of Armor – Reflection Journal

1. Identify Your Armor:

What emotional armor do you wear most often—anger, pride, control, humor, withdrawal?

2. Cost of Protection:

What relationships or opportunities have you lost because of this armor?

3. Safe Space Exploration:

Who in your life helps you feel safe enough to lower your guard? How can you deepen that trust?

4. Releasing Ritual:

Write a symbolic act of release—what would it mean to "lay down" your armor?

CHAPTER 5

Self-Esteem

"I praise You because I am fearfully and wonderfully made."— Psalm 139:14 (NIV)

Affirmation:
I am enough—without comparison,
competition, or permission.

Self-esteem is the foundation of how we see ourselves and how we show up in relationships. It shapes our confidence, our choices, and even the way we allow others to treat us.

For many of us, the story of our self-esteem begins in childhood. The words spoken to us—or withheld from us—become the inner voice we carry into adulthood.

Early Lessons in Worth

The early stages of self-esteem begin at home. Parents, caregivers, and early experiences are the first mirrors that tell a child who they are. Encouragement, love, and attention build confidence. Neglect, abuse, or constant criticism tear it down.

Think about your earliest memories of being praised—or being shamed. Did you feel seen and valued? Or did you feel invisible, unwanted, or not good enough? These moments matter more than we realize.

I grew up in a neighborhood where many parents were stretched thin—working long hours, stressed by poverty, or battling their own traumas. In those homes, frustration often came out as yelling, name-calling, or even physical abuse. What kids learned in those moments was not discipline—it was shame.

When Parents Project Their Pain

I once knew a young woman who was brilliant—top of her class, with scholarship offers and a bright future. But she got pregnant in her senior year, and her parents, overwhelmed by poverty, made her feel as though her baby ruined her life.

Instead of supporting her, they projected resentment onto her. They called her stupid, ugly, and unworthy. She eventually passed those same words onto her own child. That little girl grew up with shattered confidence, carrying the burden of her mother's unhealed pain.

This is how low self-esteem becomes generational—passed down like an inheritance no one asked for.

My Own Family Lessons

I also saw how the absence of a father can shape self-esteem. A cousin of mine grew up surrounded only by women. Without a male role model, he picked up feminine traits, which led to teasing and rejection from other kids. Even his own father assumed he was "different" and rejected him. To this day, he struggles with confidence because he has never felt accepted for who he truly is.

On the other hand, I witnessed how unconditional love can be a shield. My mother, despite her struggles, poured love into me. She wasn't perfect—she had her own battles—but her love gave me something to hold onto when the world tried to tear me down.

The Influence of Society

Self-esteem doesn't just come from family—it's shaped by society too. Television, social media, and culture constantly bombard us with false standards of beauty, success, and worth.

Children and teens compare themselves to images that aren't even real—airbrushed bodies, fake lifestyles, and material possessions. Without a strong foundation at home, many kids grow up believing they'll never measure up.

That's why conscious parenting matters. Parents must be intentional about the messages they send, teaching children that their value is not tied to looks, likes, or labels.

Breaking the Cycle

Low self-esteem isn't just painful—it's dangerous. It leads people to settle for toxic relationships, to accept abuse as love, or to sabotage opportunities because they don't feel worthy of success.

Healing self-esteem begins with awareness. It requires us to challenge the lies we were told and replace them with the truth. Instead of hearing *"You're not enough,"* we must begin saying, *"I am enough."*

Practical steps to rebuild self-esteem include:

1. **Affirm yourself daily.** Speak positive truths out loud, even if you don't fully believe them yet.
2. **Set boundaries.** Show yourself that your worth demands respect.
3. **Celebrate progress.** Focus not only on what you haven't achieved but on how far you've already come.
4. **Surround yourself with encouragers.** Distance yourself from voices that tear you down.

Reflection for the Reader

- What were the earliest messages you received about yourself?
- How did those messages shape your confidence and choices today?
- Do you find yourself repeating negative self-talk that came from parents, teachers, or peers?
- What daily practices could help you rewrite the story of your self-esteem?

Closing Thought

Self-esteem is not about arrogance—it's about acceptance. It's about believing you are enough, even as you grow.

If you grew up in shame or neglect, hear me clearly: you are not the names people called you. You are not the product of your parents' pain. You are worthy of love, respect, and success. Healing begins when you choose to see yourself as valuable—because you are.

Self-Esteem – Reflection Journal

1. Inner Voice Audit:

Write down five recurring thoughts you have about yourself. Which come from love—and which come from fear?

2. Childhood Messages:

Whose voice shaped your self-esteem the most, and what messages did they send?

3. Self-Affirmation:

Write three truths you want to start believing about your worth.

4. Daily Practice:

Create a simple 3-minute morning routine that honors your values before you face the day.

CHAPTER 6

Trust and Faith

"Faith is taking the first step even when you don't see the whole staircase." — Dr. Martin Luther King, Jr.

Affirmation:
I trust the process,
even when I cannot predict the outcome.

Trust and faith are two of the most important foundations of any relationship. Without them, love cannot survive, and healing cannot take root. Trust grounds us in honesty and security. Faith allows us to believe in what we cannot see, to hope for what is not yet here.

Trust Begins Within

Before we can trust others, we must first learn to trust ourselves. That means being honest about who we are, what we want, and how we show up in relationships.

Growing up in a poverty-stricken community, trust was fragile. Sometimes you couldn't even trust family. Broken promises, betrayal, and deceit were everywhere. As a child, I learned quickly that appearances could fool you. Couples who looked happy often lived in lies. Friends I depended on let me down. These experiences hardened me and made trust feel dangerous.

By the time I entered adulthood, I was guarded. Letting someone close meant giving them power to hurt me—and I didn't want to risk that. But I've learned that living without trust isn't really living. Without it, every relationship becomes a battlefield, and every connection eventually collapses.

The Levels of Trust

Trust isn't all-or-nothing. It builds in layers. For some, it starts with small things—sharing a phone number, venting about a bad day, or borrowing a few dollars. With time, those small acts grow into bigger ones: inviting someone into your home, sharing secrets, and making life-changing decisions together.

Every relationship—friendships, family, romance—requires patience to build trust. It can't be forced. It has to be earned, little by little. And here's the truth: once trust is lost, it may never return the same way. Broken trust creates distance, secrecy, and doubt. Sometimes forgiveness is possible. But even then, rebuilding requires humility, consistency, and proof of change.

My Personal Struggles with Trust

For me, trust has always been complicated. My lifestyle before incarceration made me suspicious of everyone's motives. In my neighborhood, giving someone your location could cost you your life. Betrayal wasn't just emotional—it could be fatal.

Even with women I cared about, I often searched for flaws, convinced they would hurt me. That suspicion pushed good people away and kept me stuck in cycles of disappointment. I had to learn that not everyone is out to betray you. Some people are worthy of trust—but you'll never know if you refuse to give them the chance.

Faith: Believing Without Proof

If trust is about people, faith is about God and the unseen. Faith means choosing to believe even when you don't have all the answers. It means knowing storms will come but also believing they won't last forever.

Faith doesn't erase fear. It gives us the courage to face our fears. It reminds us that we are not in control of everything—and that's okay.

For me, faith has been my lifeline. In my darkest moments—in depression, betrayal, and incarceration—it was faith that kept me standing. I believe God has a plan bigger than my pain. And I believe He will place the right people, opportunities, and relationships in my life when the time is right.

Trust and Faith in Relationships

In relationships, trust and faith are inseparable. You have to trust that your partner is loyal, honest, and genuine. And you have to have faith that even in hard times, your bond can survive.

Without trust, you'll live in paranoia—snooping through phones, second-guessing words, expecting betrayal. Without faith, you'll quit too soon, believing things can never get better.

Both trust and faith require vulnerability. They ask us to risk being hurt. But they also give us the only chance to experience real love.

Reflection for the Reader

- Who broke your trust in the past, and how has that shaped the way you trust now?
- Do you find yourself withholding trust out of fear?
- How do you define faith in your own life—spiritual, relational, or both?
- Are you willing to risk vulnerability to experience deeper love and connection?

Closing Thought

Trust and faith are choices we make daily. They are fragile but powerful. They require patience, honesty, and courage. And when built on a foundation of love and respect, they create the safety every relationship needs to thrive.

If you've lost trust before, don't give up. If you've struggled with faith, keep believing. Healing relationships begin when we decide to trust wisely and to live by faith—even when we can't see the outcome.

Trust and Faith – Reflection Journal

1. Trust Inventory:

Who do you currently trust, and why? Who have you stopped trusting—and what happened?

2. Self-Trust Check:

When was the last time you ignored your intuition? What was the cost?

3. Faith Anchor:

Describe a time when faith carried you through something you didn't understand.

4. Forgiveness & Rebuilding:

Who or what do you need to forgive to rebuild your capacity to trust?

CHAPTER 7

Food for Thought

"And let us not be weary in well doing: for in due season we shall reap, if we faint not." — Galatians 6:9 (KJV)

Affirmation:
My failures are not my identity—they are my teachers.

Mistakes and failures do not define us. What defines us is how we respond to them. Too often, we let bad decisions or setbacks convince us that we are unworthy, unloved, or broken beyond repair. But failure is not final—it is feedback. It's a teacher, not a life sentence.

Redefining Strength

When we go through pain, it's easy to see it only as suffering. But strength is born in pain. Strength is not about how much weight you can lift—it's about how much hardship you can endure and still keep moving forward.

To me, strength is patience when everything inside you wants to rush. Strength is faith when doubt is screaming in your ear. Strength is humility when pride tempts you to lash out.

Growing up in poverty, I saw kids who were strong in ways most people could never imagine. Their strength came from surviving circumstances that would have broken others. That taught me that strength is not about power or control—it's about resilience.

Healing from Discouragement

When relationships fail, discouragement can creep in. You start to believe that maybe you're the problem, or that you'll never find love that lasts. But discouragement is a lie.

Instead of letting failed relationships define you, let them refine you. Every breakup, every disappointment, every betrayal carries a lesson. The question is not *"Why did this happen to me?"* but *"What can I learn from this?"*

Discouragement says you're not good enough. Courage says keep trying. Keep working on yourself. Keep showing up for love. No one finds their soulmate on the first try—and if they did, they are the rare exception. For the rest of us, love is a journey of growth and discovery.

The Power of Perspective

So much of healing comes down to perspective. Negative thoughts create negative lives. If you dwell on hurt, betrayal, and rejection, you will live in bitterness. But if you shift your perspective—even slightly—you begin to see hope.

I used to expect the worst in every situation. That way, I thought I'd never be disappointed. But in reality, that mindset made me paranoid, mistrustful, and closed off. I was sabotaging my own peace.

When I began to replace negative thoughts with positive ones, everything shifted. Speaking life over yourself, even in dark places, is a form of healing. The words you repeat to yourself eventually become your reality.

Trusting God's Timing

Another trap we fall into is impatience. We want love, success, and healing on *our* timeline. But God's plan is bigger than ours. He allows delays, not to punish us, but to prepare us.

Every blessing I ever rushed into—relationships, money, opportunities—ended up hurting me. Every blessing I trusted God with came at the right time and with peace. Healing is no different. You can't force it. You can only walk in patience, trusting that every step forward brings you closer to peace.

Reflection for the Reader

- How do you define strength in your own life? Is it patience, endurance, humility, or something else?

- When you face setbacks, do you see them as failures or as lessons?
- What negative thought patterns do you need to replace with positive truths?
- Where in your life do you need more patience with God's timing?

Closing Thought

Pain, discouragement, and failure are not the end of your story. They are stepping stones toward wisdom, resilience, and peace. Your mistakes don't make you worthless—they make you human.

When you shift your perspective, pain becomes purpose. When you walk with courage, discouragement becomes growth. And when you trust God's timing, healing becomes inevitable.

Remember: the only thing stronger than your pain is the strength that grows from it.

Food for Thought – Reflection Journal

1. Redefining Strength:

What does strength mean to you today, and how has that definition evolved?

2. Learning from Loss:

List three painful moments that taught you the most about yourself.

3. Reframe Practice:

Take one discouraging situation and write how it could serve as preparation for something greater.

4. Patience Meditation:

What does "trusting God's timing" look like in your daily life?

CHAPTER 8

Boundaries, Friends, and Foundations

"Daring to set boundaries is about having the courage to love ourselves, even when we risk disappointing others." — Brené Brown

Affirmation:
My boundaries protect my peace, not my pride.

Every relationship—whether it's family, friendship, or romance—needs structure. Without boundaries, without a solid foundation, relationships collapse under the weight of confusion, disrespect, and unmet expectations.

Healing requires that we become intentional about how we build connections. Boundaries define how people treat us. Foundations determine whether the relationship can survive storms. And friendships remind us that not every bond is meant to be romantic—some are meant to anchor us in trust and support.

Building a Solid Foundation

Think of a relationship like a house. No matter how beautiful the design, if the foundation is weak, the house won't stand. In the same way, relationships built on lust, lies, or convenience will eventually fall apart.

In the past, I rushed into relationships without laying the foundation of trust, respect, and friendship. Every time, those relationships crumbled. Looking back, it wasn't bad luck—it was poor construction.

A solid foundation is built on honesty, shared values, and patience. It requires us to drop our baggage before we enter something new. Too often, we carry past hurts into new relationships, punishing people for things they never did. Healing begins when we give new relationships a fresh start.

The Importance of Boundaries

Boundaries are not walls to keep people out. They are guidelines that teach people how to love and respect us. Without them, people will push limits, often unintentionally.

When you clearly state what you will and will not accept—dishonesty, disrespect, betrayal—you empower yourself and set the tone for how others treat you.

In my younger days, I barely had boundaries. I might tell a woman not to hang up on me or not to call me names, but beyond that, I left too much room for disrespect. When you don't establish boundaries, you invite chaos. A lack of boundaries tells others, *"Do whatever you want—I'll tolerate it."*

True boundaries say: *"I know my worth. If you want to be in my life, respect it."*

Friendships: The First Test of Trust

Friendship is the foundation of every healthy relationship. Before love, before intimacy, before commitment—there should be friendship. Why? Because friendship reveals character.

Friends show you how someone listens, treats others, handles disagreements, and shows up when life gets hard. Skipping friendship and rushing into romance leaves you blind to these truths.

I used to confuse associates with friends. Associates are people you spend time with, maybe share laughs or experiences. Friends are those you trust with your secrets, your struggles, and your growth. Associates may clap when you win, but friends stand with you when you lose.

Learning the difference saved me a lot of pain.

Questions to Ask Yourself About Friendship

- What does "friend" mean to you?
- Do you trust your friends the same way you trust your family—or more?
- What are your expectations of a true friend?
- Do you separate associates from real friends, or do you let everyone in the same circle?

Answering these questions honestly helps you recognize who belongs in your inner circle. Not everyone who calls you "bro," "sis," or "best friend" has earned that title.

Communication and Conflict

Friendship, like any relationship, is tested in conflict. The question is not whether you'll disagree—it's how you handle it.

Growing up with a street mentality, disagreements often turned into fights. That was all I knew. But I learned that healthy communication—listening, speaking respectfully, and seeking understanding—is what separates lasting friendships from temporary ones.

When we communicate with aggression, we destroy trust. When we communicate with patience and respect, we strengthen it.

Reflection for the Reader

- Do you set clear boundaries in your relationships, or do you let things slide?
- Are your current relationships built on solid foundations or on shaky ground?
- Who in your life is a true friend, and who is only an associate?
- How do you handle disagreements—with aggression, avoidance, or understanding?

Closing Thought

Relationships don't fail because love disappears. They fail because they were never built on trust, respect, and clear boundaries. If you want healthy connections, start by being intentional. Build strong foundations. Set boundaries. Choose friends wisely. When you do, you'll find that relationships stop draining you and start strengthening you.

Boundaries, Friends, and Foundations – Reflection

1. Boundary Blueprint:

What are three non-negotiable boundaries you need in your relationships right now?

2. Friendship Audit:

List your five closest relationships. Which of them truly pour into you—and which drain you?

3. Foundation Check:

Think of one relationship built on shaky ground. What would it take to rebuild or release it?

4. Communication Practice:

Write a short statement you could use in your next conflict that expresses truth without hostility.

CHAPTER 9

The Effect of Sex

"Do you not know that your bodies are temples of the Holy Spirit... You are not your own?" — 1 Corinthians 6:19 (NIV)

Affirmation:
My body is sacred. My love is divine. I will honor both.

Sex is one of the most powerful forces in relationships, but also one of the most misunderstood. When treated as sacred, it can strengthen intimacy. When treated carelessly, it can destroy trust, self-worth, and even identity.

Many people build entire relationships on sex, confusing physical pleasure with emotional connection. But when sex becomes the foundation, the relationship almost always collapses. Flesh may satisfy for a moment, but it cannot carry the weight of love, loyalty, or respect.

My Own Misunderstanding of Sex

When I was young, I thought the more women I slept with, the more respect I earned. The neighborhood I grew up in praised promiscuity. The streets taught me that having multiple women meant power, status, and pride.

But looking back, I see how destructive that mindset was—not only to the women I used, but also to myself. I left women hurt and confused, cutting off contact without explanation. In my immaturity, I thought it didn't matter. But sex is never *just* sex. When you give your body to someone, you give them a piece of yourself. Over time, those pieces add up, leaving you drained, confused, and often broken.

The Cost of Casual Sex

Casual sex creates false connections. One person may believe it's just physical, while the other develops emotional attachment. When the expectations don't match, pain follows.

For many, casual sex also leads to low self-esteem. Each time you give your body away without real intimacy, you risk feeling used, unworthy, or disposable. You start to question your value, wondering if people want you for who you are—or only for what you can offer physically.

Sex is sacred. It is not meant to be cheapened. Just as you would protect a valuable possession or a luxury car, your body deserves to be cherished, respected, and handled with care.

A Message to Women and Young Queens

I have four nieces and thinking about them changed how I view sex and women. Society often pressures women to lead with sex, whether on social media, in entertainment, or in relationships. But queens don't have to sell themselves short.

Respect yourself first, and others will follow your lead. The way you carry yourself determines how people approach you. If you act like you are priceless, people will treat you that way. If you act like you are disposable, some will gladly take advantage of you.

You are not an object. You are not a trophy. You are not a body to be conquered. You are a queen, deserving of devotion, respect, and love.

Sex and Self-Esteem

Sex also affects how men see themselves. Many men, like me, use sex as a distraction from emptiness. We chase intimacy with our bodies because we are afraid of intimacy with our emotions. We confuse lust for love, and when lust fades, we feel emptier than before.

True healing requires us to stop using sex as medicine for wounds that it cannot heal. Until we confront the real pain—trauma, rejection, loneliness—we will continue to repeat the cycle.

Reflection for the Reader

- Do you view sex as sacred or casual?
- Have you ever tied your self-worth to sexual attention?

- Do your relationships rely more on physical connection than emotional trust and respect?
- What would it look like to treat your body—and your partner's body—as sacred?

Closing Thought

Sex can bring two people closer, but it can also tear them apart. Its effect depends on how we value ourselves and our partners.

If you want real love, don't build it on flesh alone. Build it on respect, honesty, trust, and friendship. When sex is rooted in love and purpose, it becomes a powerful expression of intimacy. But when it's misused, it leaves scars.

Treat your body like the temple it is. Demand respect. Protect your worth. And remember: sex may touch the body, but love heals the soul.

The Effect of Sex – Reflection Journal

1. Self-Worth and Intimacy:

Have you ever used sex to feel validated or loved? What emotions were you avoiding at that time?

2. Sacredness Reclaimed:

What does “sex as sacred” mean to you personally?

3. Emotional Connection:

How do you want to feel after intimacy—and what boundaries ensure that?

4. Body as Temple:

Write a declaration affirming your body as sacred and worthy of care.

CHAPTER 10

Trust and Faith — The Glue of Relationships

"Love is an act of endless forgiveness, a tender look which becomes a habit."— Peter Ustinov

Affirmation:
I choose to love with wisdom, to trust with grace, and to believe with courage.

Every relationship requires many ingredients—love, respect, communication—but two stand above all: **trust and faith.** These are the glue that holds everything together. Without trust, love withers. Without faith, hope dies. And without both, no relationship can survive.

The Fragility of Trust

Trust is like glass—once broken, it can be repaired, but the cracks always remain.

I used to believe trust could be demanded. If someone loved me, they should trust me no matter what. But I learned the hard way that trust is not a gift—it's a responsibility. It must be earned through consistency, honesty, and transparency.

When I lied to women, I lost their trust. When I cheated, I shattered it completely. And when I betrayed myself through poor choices, I lost trust in myself, too. Rebuilding trust is harder than building it the first time. It takes patience, humility, and proof.

Faith: The Anchor in Storms

If trust is built between people, faith is built between people and God. Relationships will be tested by financial struggles, temptation, health issues, distance, or personal insecurities. Without faith, those storms feel unbearable. With faith, they become opportunities for growth.

Faith reminds us that no relationship is perfect and that every bond requires forgiveness, grace, and endurance. It gives us the courage to love even when it's risky, to stay even when it's hard, and to believe even when hope feels faint.

Lessons From My Own Journey

My own brokenness showed me the danger of living without trust or faith. I chased relationships without boundaries, disrespected women I cared about, and let suspicion poison my connections.

Looking back, I realize the real issue wasn't the women I dated—it was me. I didn't trust myself, so I couldn't fully trust anyone else. I didn't have faith in my own healing, so I couldn't have faith in lasting love.

Once I began my journey of healing, everything shifted. I started to understand that:

- Trust is built slowly, but it can be lost instantly.
- Faith is tested most in the dark, but it shines brightest there.
- Both require vulnerability—risking pain in order to experience love.

Practical Principles for Trust and Faith in Relationships

1. **Be Transparent.** Secrets erode trust. Share openly and honestly.
2. **Keep Your Word.** Small promises matter. Follow through.
3. **Forgive, But Don't Forget.** Forgiveness is healing, but boundaries are wisdom.
4. **Pray Together.** Faith grows stronger when it's shared.
5. **Trust Yourself First.** You can't offer others what you haven't built within.

Reflection for the Reader

- Who in your life has broken your trust, and how has that shaped you?

- Do you find yourself expecting betrayal instead of believing in honesty?
- How do you lean on faith when relationships are tested?
- What step could you take this week to rebuild trust—with yourself, with God, or with someone you love?

Closing Thought

Trust and faith are not luxuries—they are necessities. They are what allow love to grow roots and survive the storms of life. Without them, relationships collapse under suspicion, fear, and hopelessness.

But when you choose trust—when you give faith a chance—you open the door to healing, intimacy, and real love.

Remember this: trust is the soil, faith is the water, and love is the seed. Together, they create relationships that can stand the test of time.

Trust and Faith—The Glue of Relationships – Reflection Journal

1. Broken Glass Moments:

When has trust been broken in your life? What have those moments taught you about honesty and repair?

2. Faith Under Fire:

How do you maintain faith when love feels uncertain or when people fail you?

3. Action Step:

What one action can you take this week to demonstrate trustworthiness—to yourself or to someone else?

4. Gratitude & Growth:

List three ways your faith has already helped you grow beyond what once broke you.

CONCLUSION

The Journey Toward Wholeness

"For I know the plans I have for you... plans to give you hope and a future." —Jeremiah 29:11 (NIV)

Affirmation:
My scars are sacred—they remind me that I survived.

Healing is not a destination. It is a lifelong journey—a winding road of facing truth, letting go of pain, and choosing growth over stagnation. As we close this book, I want to take a step back and reflect on everything we have walked through together.

This is not just my story. It is a story of humanity. It is a story of brokenness and resilience, of wounds and redemption, of fear and faith. And it is a story that, in one way or another, belongs to all of us.

The Scars of Childhood Trauma

Our journey began in childhood. Many of us are carrying wounds we did not choose. Trauma—whether through abuse, neglect, abandonment, or loss—shapes how we see ourselves and how we interact with the world.

I know what it means to carry scars from a young age. To be touched in ways that were wrong. To watch family members struggle with addiction. To bury loved ones before understanding what death even meant. Those experiences do not just disappear when we become adults. They live in us—whispering lies about who we are and what we deserve.

But here's the truth: your trauma is not your identity. It is part of your story, but it does not define your future. Healing requires us to confront those early wounds, to name them, and to strip them of their power. When we stop running from our past, we gain the strength to reclaim our future.

Brokenness and the Lies We Believe

We then moved into the reality of being broken. Brokenness does not come only from what others do to us—it comes from the choices we make when we are hurting.

I tied my worth to money, women, and status. When I lost money, I felt worthless. When I lost relationships, I felt unlovable. Depression whispered lies until I considered ending my life.

Being broken is not about weakness. It is about being human. We all have moments when life knocks us down so hard that we wonder if we will ever stand again. But brokenness is also where transformation begins. Just as a seed must break open before it grows, we, too, must break open to become who we were meant to be.

The Beginning of Healing

Healing starts with honesty. It starts with admitting that something is wrong. It starts with accountability—taking responsibility for the choices we made, even while acknowledging the pain we didn't choose.

Healing is like a butterfly's cocoon. It is uncomfortable. It requires isolation, patience, and surrender. But without it, we never become who we are destined to be.

For me, healing meant facing my pride, letting go of blame, and rebuilding my faith in God. For you, it may mean therapy, prayer, journaling, or forgiveness. Whatever the path, the truth remains: healing is possible, but it requires commitment.

The Armor We Wear

As we journeyed further, we explored the armor we wear to survive. Anger, pride, numbness, toughness—these shields protect us temporarily, but they also weigh us down.

I wore armor to keep people from seeing my pain. But armor doesn't just keep pain out—it keeps love out too. True healing requires us to lay it down, piece by piece, and allow ourselves to be vulnerable again. Vulnerability is not weakness. It is courage in its purest form.

Self-Esteem: The Foundation of Identity

Low self-esteem is one of the greatest enemies of healing. When you don't see yourself as valuable, you settle for relationships that diminish you, jobs that underpay you, and environments that drain you.

Self-esteem is not arrogance—it is acceptance. It is the quiet confidence of knowing: *I am worthy of love, respect, and peace.*

To build healthy self-esteem, you must challenge the lies of your past and replace them with truth. You must surround yourself with people who uplift you, not people who tear you down. And you must learn to celebrate progress, even when perfection feels far away.

Trust and Faith: The Glue of Relationships

Relationships cannot thrive without trust and faith. Trust is earned through consistency, and faith is sustained through belief—in God, in ourselves, and in others.

I learned the hard way what broken trust looks like. Lies, cheating, betrayal—they destroy relationships from the inside out. But I also learned that without faith, relationships cannot endure storms. Faith allows us to keep going even when things get hard. It anchors us when everything else feels uncertain.

Trust and faith require vulnerability. They ask us to risk being hurt in order to experience real love. And while that risk is frightening, it is the only way to build connections that last.

Sex and Sacredness

One of the most misunderstood aspects of relationships is sex. I grew up believing sex was proof of power, popularity, and pride. But in reality, it was a false escape from emptiness.

Sex is sacred. It is more than physical—it is spiritual and emotional. When misused, it can damage self-worth and create toxic cycles. But when honored, it deepens intimacy and strengthens bonds.

True healing requires us to view our bodies—and the bodies of others—as temples of value, not objects of conquest. Your worth is not tied to your sexuality. Your worth is tied to who you are as a whole person.

Food for Thought: Lessons from the Struggle

Life has a way of teaching us through struggle. Every failure carries a lesson. Every heartbreak carries a seed of wisdom. Every setback prepares us for a comeback.

The key is perspective. If you see every failure as final, you will live in despair. But if you see every failure as feedback, you will live in a state of growth. Healing is not about avoiding pain—it is about learning from it.

Boundaries and Foundations

Healthy relationships require boundaries and strong foundations. Without boundaries, we invite chaos. Without foundations, we collapse at the first storm.

Boundaries teach people how to love us. Foundations anchor relationships in honesty, respect, and patience. And friendships remind us that not every relationship needs romance—some need loyalty, trust, and support.

When you set boundaries, you honor yourself. When you build on solid foundations, you honor the relationship.

The Call to Action: Healing Yourself First

Every chapter of this book comes back to one truth: you cannot heal relationships without first healing yourself.

You cannot love others if you do not love yourself. You cannot trust others if you do not trust yourself. You cannot build healthy connections if your foundation is still cracked by unhealed trauma.

Healing yourself first is not selfish—it is necessary. It is how you break generational curses. It is how you stop cycles of abuse, betrayal, and neglect. It is how you create relationships that thrive instead of survive.

Where Do We Go From Here?

So where do we go from here?

We go forward—with honesty. With courage. With faith.

We commit to the daily work of healing, even when it's uncomfortable. We forgive ourselves for the mistakes we've made. We hold ourselves accountable for the choices we can control. We surround ourselves with people who pour into us rather than drain us. We put God at the center of our relationships, trusting Him to guide us when we falter.

Healing is not a one-time decision—it is a lifestyle.

Final Reflections for the Reader

As you close this book, I invite you to reflect:

- What pieces of armor are you still carrying, and are you ready to lay them down?
- What lies about your worth are you still believing, and how can you replace them with truth?
- What boundaries do you need to set to protect your peace?
- Where do you need to rebuild trust—with yourself, with God, or with others?
- And most importantly, are you willing to begin your healing journey today—not tomorrow, not when life feels easier, but today?

Closing Thought

My story began in brokenness, but it does not end there. And neither does yours. You are not your trauma. You are not your mistakes. You are not your brokenness. You are a child of God, worthy of healing, worthy of love, worthy of peace.

The chapters of this book may be ending, but your story is still being written. And with every choice you make toward healing, you are writing a story of resilience, redemption, and hope.

So, walk forward—scarred but stronger, wounded but wiser, imperfect but still worthy. Healing is not just possible. It is promised if you are willing to do the work. And remember this: **the greatest gift you can give to yourself, and to the people you love, is a healed you.**

The Journey Toward Wholeness – Reflection Journal

1. Integration:

What themes throughout this book resonated most with your own story?

2. Wholeness Vision:

Describe what a healed version of you looks, sounds, and feels like.

3. Daily Healing Habit:

What one small act will you commit to doing every day to stay aligned with your healing?

4. Final Affirmation:

Write a closing statement of power beginning with: *"I am not my pain..."*

About the Author

J. **Love** is a man whose life story embodies the power of redemption, resilience, and spiritual awakening. Born into an environment shaped by poverty, addiction, and violence, he witnessed pain and loss at an early age. His childhood was marked by trauma, abuse, and instability—experiences that left invisible scars and shaped the path he would later walk.

Like many young men seeking a sense of belonging, he turned to the streets for identity and validation. The lessons he learned there were hard, and the consequences were harder. Years of pain, broken relationships, and incarceration became both his classroom and his crucible. It was in his darkest moments—alone, stripped of freedom and illusion—that he began the most important journey of his life: the journey inward.

Behind prison walls, he discovered what the world could not teach him—**that true healing begins with honesty, accountability, and faith.** Through prayer, study, and reflection, he began confronting the roots of his pain: childhood trauma, unhealed grief, misplaced identity, and self-sabotage. In that sacred space of stillness, he found God, purpose, and peace.

Chains to Change: Breaking Trauma and Building Healthy Relationships was born from that transformation. It is not a book about perfection—it is a book about process. Through raw storytelling and spiritual insight, the author invites readers to see that no matter how deep the wound, healing is still possible. His reflections on trauma, love, trust, sex, and faith are deeply human, reminding us that freedom is not found in escape, but in self-awareness and surrender.

Today, his life's mission is to inspire others—especially men and women carrying silent pain—to confront their truth, embrace their worth, and walk in healing. He is not only a survivor of trauma but a messenger of restoration. His work speaks to those who feel forgotten, those who have made mistakes, and those who are ready to transform pain into purpose.

When he is not writing, mentoring, or speaking, he continues to serve as a beacon of hope for individuals seeking faith-based healing and personal growth. His message is simple but profound:

"You are not your past. You are not your mistakes. You are not your pain. You are proof that God still heals broken things."

Through his words, his wisdom, and his witness, **J. Love** stands as living proof that even the heaviest chains can be transformed into change.

www.ingramcontent.com/pod-product-compliance
Lightning Source LLC
LaVergne TN
LVHW090614110826
845146LV00001B/384

* 9 7 9 8 9 9 5 3 2 7 2 1 9 *